Here are insights from the teaching of Jesus, whose words of wisdom turned conventional thinking upside-down, and brought hope and new life to a troubled world.

This selection is illustrated with graphic, contemporary images — and, for those who like to collect quotations, there are hidden truths, words of wisdom, power and promise beneath the extra leaf on each page.

I N S I G H T S

FROM · THE · TEACHING · OF · JESUS

A LION BOOK

Tring · Batavia · Sydney

KINGDOM

The Spirit of the Lord is upon me; he has appointed me to preach Good News to the poor; he has sent me to announce that captives shall be released and the blind shall see, that the downtrodden shall be freed from their oppressors, and that God is ready to give blessings to all who come to him.

L I F E

If anyone is thirsty, let him come to me and drink. For the Scriptures declare that rivers of living water shall flow from the inmost being of anyone who believes in me.

WORRY

Do not worry about your life, what you will eat; or about your body, what you will wear. Life is more than food, and the body more than clothes. Consider the ravens: they do not sow or reap, they have no storeroom or barn; yet God feeds them. And how much more valuable you are than birds! Who of you by worrying can add a single hour to his life? Since you cannot do this very little thing, why do you worry about the rest?

Consider how the lilies grow. They do not labour or spin. Yet I tell you, not even Solomon in all his splendour was dressed like one of these. If that is how God clothes the grass of the field, which is here today, and tomorrow is thrown into the fire, how much more will he clothe you, O you of little faith?

L OVE

'Love the Lord your God with all your heart, soul, and mind.'
This is the first and greatest commandment. The second most
important is similar: 'Love your neighbour as much as you love
yourself.'

Love your enemies, do good to those who hate you, bless those
who curse you, and pray for those who ill-treat you. If anyone
hits you on one cheek, let him hit the other one too; if someone
takes your coat, let him have your shirt as well. Give to
everyone who asks you for something, and when someone
takes what is yours, do not ask for it back. Do for others just
what you want them to do for you . . . Do not judge others, and
God will not judge you; do not condemn others, and God will
not condemn you; forgive others, and God will forgive you.

TREASURE

Do not store up riches for yourselves here on earth, where moths and rust destroy, and robbers break in and steal. Instead, store up riches for yourselves in heaven, where moths and rust cannot destroy, and robbers cannot break in and steal. For your heart will always be where your riches are.

THE TRUE LAW

You have heard that it was said to the people long ago, 'Do not murder, and anyone who murders will be subject to judgment.' But I tell you that anyone who is angry with his brother will be subject to judgment.

You have heard that it was said, 'Do not commit adultery.' But I tell you that anyone who looks at a woman lustfully has already committed adultery with her in his heart.

W ISDOM

Not every one who says to me, 'Lord, Lord,' shall enter the Kingdom of heaven, but he who does the will of my Father who is in heaven . . . Everyone then who hears these words of mine and does them will be like a wise man who built his house upon the rock; and the rain fell, and the floods came, and the winds blew and beat upon that house, but it did not fall, because it had been founded on a rock. And everyone who hears these words of mine and does not do them will be like a foolish man who built his house upon the sand; and the rain fell, and the floods came, and the winds blew and beat against that house, and it fell; and great was the fall of it.

$\boxed{\text{B}}$ E Y O N D $\boxed{\text{D}}$ E A T H

Do not let your hearts be troubled. Trust in God; trust also in me. In my Father's house are many rooms; if it were not so, I would have told you. I am going there to prepare a place for you.

ETERNAL LIFE

God loved the world so much that he gave his only Son so that anyone who believes in him shall not perish but have eternal life. God did not send his Son into the world to condemn it, but to save it.

Copyright © 1988 Lion Publishing

Published by
Lion Publishing plc
Icknield Way, Tring, Herts, England
ISBN 0 7459 1331 8

Albatross Books Pty Ltd
PO Box 320, Sutherland, NSW 2232, Australia
ISBN 0 86760 893 5

First edition 1988

Acknowledgments
All photographs are by ZEFA (UK) Ltd except *Kingdom* which is by Lion
Publishing: David Townsend.

Bible quotations are taken from *Good News Bible*, copyright 1966, 1971
and 1976 American Bible Society, published by the Bible Societies/Collins;
Holy Bible, New International Version (British edition), copyright
1978 New York International Bible Society; *The Living Bible*, copyright
1971 Tyndale House Publishers; *Revised Standard Version*, copyright
1946 and 1952, second edition 1971, Division of Christian Education,
National Council of the Churches of Christ in the USA

References in the order in which they appear, giving Gospel, chapter
and verse numbers:
Kingdom Luke 4:14–21; Matthew 13:44
True Happiness Matthew 5:1–10; John 8:12
Life John 7:37–38; John 10:10
Worry Luke 12:22–31; John 6:35
Love Matthew 22:37–39; Luke 6:27–37; Luke 6:38
Treasure Matthew 6:19–21; Luke 12:15–21
The True Law Matthew 5:21–22, 27–28; Matthew 7:13–14
Wisdom Matthew 7:21, 24-27; John 14:6
Beyond Death John 14:1–3; John 11:25–26
Eternal Life John 3:16–17; Matthew 11:28–29

British Library Cataloguing in Publication Data
[Bible. O.T. Gospels. *English. Selections 1987*]
    Insights from the teaching of Jesus.
    226'.052   BS2553
    ISBN 0-7459-1331-8

Printed and bound in Singapore